EVERY LITTLE THING

Six Small Steps to Perfect Peace

Gabriel O'Sullivan

ISBN 978-1-63814-359-8 (Paperback)
ISBN 978-1-63814-360-4 (Digital)

Copyright © 2022 Gabriel O'Sullivan
All rights reserved
First Edition

All rights reserved. No part of this publication may be reproduced, distributed, or transmitted in any form or by any means, including photocopying, recording, or other electronic or mechanical methods without the prior written permission of the publisher. For permission requests, solicit the publisher via the address below.

Covenant Books, Inc.
11661 Hwy 707
Murrells Inlet, SC 29576
www.covenantbooks.com

PROLOGUE

"What?! You got mustard on my solid white hat I let you borrow?! Come on, man! How old are you?!" I inappropriately scolded a friend of mine as he explained he had permanently damaged one of my favorite ball caps. Why do guys share hats? I'm not sure.

"Man, I'm sorry," he replied. "Let me make it up to you. I know you like my Bob Marley CD, and a new one is the same price as the hat. How about I get you one, and we will call it even?"

"Deal."

And that was how I was introduced to the song, "Three Little Birds."

A few weeks later, another friend and I were lounging on a beach in Hilton Head Island listening to my new Bob Marley and The Wailers greatest hits CD on my Jambox (Yes, Jambox. It was a thing, a very big thing back in the '80s and '90s. Look it up.), and I quickly fell in love with the abovementioned song, primarily because of the following lyrics: "Don't worry about a thing. 'Cause every little thing gonna be all right."

Cut to today.

How many times have you thought in recent days, months, or years that every little thing was *not* going to be all right? How many days have you lived your life as if it was your job to worry? I bet, a lot, and I know because I've been there too.

Considering the challenges we are facing this day and age, real and imagined, how can we live lives with peace and joy instead of fear and dread? Pandemics, job loss, injustice, political scandals, death, divorce, drugs—the list goes on. So is it really possible to live daily with the tranquility we feel at our favorite beach, hearing the gentle roar of the waves, with feet buried in sand? Can we actually heed the advice of the three little birds from the song and "don't worry about a thing"?

I think so. By the end of this book, with its six small steps, I hope you think the same.

Peace.

CHAPTER 1

Preseason Is for a Reason

> *Rejoice in the Lord always; again I will say, rejoice. Let your reasonableness be known to everyone. The Lord is at hand; do not be anxious about anything, but in everything by prayer and supplication with thanksgiving let your requests be made known to God. And the peace of God, which surpasses all understanding, will guard your hearts and minds in Christ Jesus. Finally, brothers, whatever is true, whatever is honorable, whatever is just, whatever is pure, whatever is lovely, whatever is commendable, if there is anything worthy of praise, think about these things. What you have learned and received and heard and seen in me—practice these things and the God of peace will be with you.*
> —Philippians 4:4–9

Within two and a half months, our three daughters were dead. Complications due to prematurity had taken them from us. We were devastated. The dreams we had for our lives with our triplet daughters turned into nightmares as we struggled through days and nights in the neonatal ICU of our local hospital and, eventually, the cemetery. My wife and I had both been so carefree, at peace, full of excitement, hope, and joy. Now we were shells of the people we had been—confused, angry, hopeless. How could God allow our children to suffer like they did? Why would he take them from us? What did we do to deserve this fate?

By God's grace, he allowed us not to turn to illicit behavior to numb the pain but rather to his Word. And in his Word, the verse written above struck a chord in our hearts and became very valuable to us as we navigated the months and years of emotional and spiritual recovery, realizing that even in difficulty, God has good planned for those who love him. We didn't deserve the loss of our girls, but rather, bad things sometimes happen in this broken world. However, we have the hope that God protects innocent life, and one day, we will be reunited with our girls in heaven.

Enough about us. What about you? You've either had hard times in your life, are in the midst of a challenging situation, or you will one day trudge through the mire of disillusionment, difficulty, or defeat. We will all face tough times. The question is, How will we respond? The answer often lies in our preparation, our life habits that have predated the difficulty.

Not serving in the armed forces myself, I have become enamored with the work ethic and preparation of our service men and women, particularly those in our Special Forces. A commonality I've noticed if reading articles or books, listening to podcasts, or watching documentaries is they all highlight the fact that high quality preparation before the battle is most often the determining factor in the outcome. Operators stress that repetition of encounters and tactics in an as-real-to-life environment as possible is crucial to help ensure safety of the teams and victory. We see the same concept played out with kids learning math facts or sports teams, practicing the same calculations, plays, and formations again and again and again. Why? So when the time comes to perform, the soldier, student, or athlete is competent, calm, and ready to succeed. Performance becomes second nature. Patterns of muscle and mind memory allow for proper execution.

Let's compare the above to the scripture from Philippians and to a regular person facing trying times but yearning for peace. God, through Paul, makes clear that we are to live lives constantly full of rejoicing, reasonableness (gentleness), prayer, and thanksgiving. He also gives a list of actions and attitudes that we are to emulate, and he promises that when we add all these up, we will acquire the peace of God *and* that the God of peace will be with us.

As we stroll through the sand along our journey of these pages, my hope is that we will understand and commit to practice the tactics that will give us victory over panic and lead us to peace.

CHAPTER 2

Step 1

Rejoice!

Rejoice in the Lord always; again I will say, rejoice.
—Philippians 4:9

I get it. Some days, maybe most days, you may not feel like *always* rejoicing. So how and why would a prerequisite to peace be to apparently make a conscience decision to be full of joy, be excitedly joyful? It's easy to be joyful when you get a raise, are given a gift, go on vacation, have your comment or photo liked, but it's not as easy to rejoice when your loved one gets a bad diagnosis, when your job is terminated, when your car breaks down and you don't have the money to have it repaired. Paul is not suggesting that we walk through life with a fake smile, grinning, and bearing the hardships. Some people or circumstances in life are not pleasant and will not bring happiness, but we can have an underlying sense of joy everyday. How? By understanding the benefits of being in God's family if you are a follower of Christ.

So why can followers of Christ have sustained daily joy?

Because our citizenship is in heaven.

Paul writes in Philippians 3:20, "But our citizenship is in heaven and from it we await a Savior, the Lord Jesus Christ." He goes on to write in Philippians 4:3b, in regard to those whose citizenship is in heaven, that their "names are in the book of life." What is he communicating? If one is in Christ, meaning he has given up the right to himself, has repented of sin and of placing himself as Lord of his own life, and has asked Christ to be Lord and Savior, believing Jesus is God, that Jesus came to earth as a sacrifice for our sin, died on the cross, arose after three days, and now sits on his throne in heaven, then that person in Christ has moved from being a citizen of earth to a citizen of heaven, with his name written in the book of life—the book that contains the names of those who will be allowed to live eternally with God in heaven at the end of time or the end of his earthly life. That is the reason to always be full of joy! Eternal Life! But don't take my word for it. Below are some other scriptures that cement this good news and give us reasons to have joy.

- "For God so love the world that he gave his only Son, that whoever believes in him will not perish but have *eternal life*" (John 3:16).
- "For the wages of sin is death, but the free gift of God is *eternal life* in Christ Jesus our Lord" (Romans 6:23).
- "Now to him who is able to do far more abundantly than all we can ask or think, according to the power at work within us, to him be glory in the church and in Christ Jesus throughout all generations, forever and ever Amen" (Ephesians 3:20–21).
- "But we do not want you to be uninformed, brothers, about those who are asleep that you may not grieve as others do who have no hope. For since we believe that since Jesus died and rose again even so through Jesus God will bring with him those who have fallen asleep. For this we declare to you by a word from the Lord that we who are alive, who are left until the coming of the Lord will not precede those who have fallen asleep. For the Lord himself will descend from heaven with a cry of command, with the voice of an archangel and with the sound of the trumpet of God. And the dead in Christ will rise first. Then we who are alive, who are left, will be caught up together with them in the

clouds to meet the Lord in the air, and *so we will always be with the Lord*. Therefore, encourage one another with these words" (1 Thessalonians 4:13–18).

- "But *our citizenship is in heaven*, and from it we await a Savior, the Lord Jesus Christ, who will transform our lowly body to be like his glorious body, by the power that enables him even to subject all things to himself" (Philippians 3:20–21).
- "Then I saw a new heaven and a new earth, for the first heaven and the first earth had passed away, and the sea was no more. And I saw the holy city, new Jerusalem, coming down out of heaven from God, prepared as a bride adorned for her husband. And I heard a loud voice from the throne saying, 'Behold, *the dwelling place of God is with man*, He will dwell with them, and they will be his people, and God himself will be with them as their God. He will wipe away every tear from their eyes, and death shall be no more, neither shall there be mourning, nor crying, nor pain anymore, for the former things have passed away'" (Revelation 21:1–4).
- "As the Father has loved me, so have I loved you" (John 15:9).
- "Jesus said to them, 'Peace be with you'" (John 20:21).
- "Take heart! Your sins are forgiven" (Matthew 9:2).
- "And he (Jesus) lifted up his eyes on his disciples, and said: 'Blessed are you who are poor, for yours is the kingdom of God. Blessed are you who are hungry now, for you shall be satisfied. Blessed are you who weep now, for you shall laugh'" (Luke 6:20–21).

Remember, it's difficult to be fretful when we are grateful. Living a life of joy and thankfulness leaves little to no room for fear, worry, and doubt. The words above call us to a life of thankfulness and rejoicing because of the promises we have in Christ when we have a relationship with him. Certainly we have more promises in Christ for this earth, but the scriptures above give a glimpse of why we can have exceedingly great joy. Just because we have the mental knowledge of reasons to rejoice, we must also choose to have the attitude and action of rejoicing, being joyful no matter what we are facing, remembering the reasons we have to rejoice. That is why Paul commands us two times in two sentences. We can know all the above and still choose to focus on the wrong, the bad, the ugly of this world. To have lasting peace, we must choose to set before us the goodness of the Lord, what he has done for us, and the glorious future that awaits.

CHAPTER 3

Step 2

Be Gentle

Let your reasonableness to be known to everyone. The Lord is at hand.
—Philippians 4:5

Be Gentle/Reasonable

At the time of this writing, our children are fourteen years old (daughter), nine years old (son), and four years old (son). They all love to wrestle. They start out playing and end up fighting. If you have siblings or have children of your own, I'm sure you can relate. As the playing escalates, my wife and I have to repeatedly remind the older kids to "Be gentle!" As you can imagine, our yelling at the kids to be gentle as they fight usually has zero effect, and the living room WWE match eventually ends in someone (or all!) crying. It's hard to have gentle and calm actions, attitudes, and words when life and tensions get tense.

If one is known as being unreasonable or unmanageable, that is not a compliment. Such a person is generally regarded as being one without control over his emotions, attitude, language, or actions. Gentleness of mind, spirit, or speech is not a hallmark trait of an unreasonable person. Peaceable would be the last characteristic that would be attributed to him. Yet if one is known to be reasonable or gentle, an aura of peace and quietness, kindness, and thoughtfulness permeates the air around him and is infectious to those near.

Philippians 4:5 highlights that Christians are expected to be gentle and reasonable—not just to those who agree with us, not just to those in our same sociodemographic tier, not just to those with the same skin color, not just to those from our same culture or beliefs but, rather, to *everyone*. And this same advice is good for non-Christians as well. Why? Because "the Lord is at hand," or as the NIV translates it, "the Lord is near."

We must remember that our God is always alongside us. He is all knowing and all present. It is our calling to always honor him by our thoughts, attitudes, and actions by striving to be as he is—gentle and reasonable. When our goal is to please him by rightly loving others, then our lives will be at peace because they will not be double lives. Blessing one and cursing another lead to shame, inner turmoil, feelings of unrest, and unrighteous anger. If Jesus was physically standing next to us, how would our lives and words be different? We must remember that he is always with us, in us, seeing all, knowing all, hearing all, and having our lives reflect this reality leads us to consistency. Consistency of word and deed can lead to peace.

Also consider similar scripture that evoke the ethos of gentleness. Philippians 2:4 reads, "Let each of you look not only to your own interests but also to the interest of others." When we are living with reason and a gentle spirit, our nature will be one of servanthood selflessness. When considering others' opinions, their wants, or perceived needs, we realize that being self-serving or bullheaded cannot coincide with a posture of selflessness. Certainly putting others ahead of ourselves flies in the face of the win-at-all-cost mentality and survival-of-the-fittest attitudes that seem to dominate our current culture, but this is the command of the Lord. There is nothing wrong with pushing forward in life to provide for our families or advance the Kingdom, but we tamper such aspirations with love, justice, mercy, and servanthood. In the book of Jeremiah, the Lord reminds the evil king, Jehoiakim, that his father, King Josiah, had such a long and prosperous rule, *not* because he invoked his authority and pressed the people but because he "was just and right in all his dealings" (Jeremiah 22:15). He was not a pushover. He was simply just and right. We can be gentle, reasonable, and a servant to others and still be strong while being a person of peace. Being a person of peace helps usher in more people of peace to our circles of influence and affects and fills us with more feelings of gentleness and calm.

The Lord Is at Hand

Remember, God is always near. He is everywhere all the time, yet at the same time, he is enthroned in heaven, and one day, "like a thief in the night," will come back to call his own to heaven and judge the world. This realization should bring to our minds the understanding that we are to not think more highly of ourselves than we ought, and we should cast off any entitlement mentality. There is no reason for a believer to feel entitled to anything. We are not king. Jesus is king, and if our Lord Jesus had "no place to lay his head," then why should we feel like we are owed anything by anyone? What right do we have to be harsh or unreasonable?

Read the words of Jesus recorded in Luke 14:8–9: "When you are invited by someone to a wedding feast, do not sit down in a place of honor, lest someone more distinguished than you be invited by him, and he who invited you both will come and say to you, 'Give your place to this person,' and then you will begin with shame to take the lowest place." Jesus reminds us to approach all situations with a humbleness of spirit and mind, realizing that if we do the opposite, there is a chance we will be humbled, not of our own accord.

Those who go through life with a sense that the world owes them honor, prestige, or respect live with an attitude of haughtiness, disdain, and anger. They are constantly under pressure to be perceived in a high light, and when they are not given the respect they think they are owed, their attitude and actions often become unmanageable. Not only so, but this person will have an anxious spirit, anticipating the next slight from whomever, wherever. We see this played out simply driving down the street, motorists yelling behind their windshields at whoever dares cut them off or drive too slowly in the left lane—not to mention in families, businesses, government, and, unfortunately, some churches. Where's the peace in such a mindset? Conversely if one travels through life with a spirit of humility, then when blessings and honor come, she is joyous to have received such an unexpected gift, not puffed up because the accolade was demanded or expected.

Consider the words penned by Paul to the Church at Philippi:

> Have this mind among yourselves, which is yours in Christ Jesus, who, though he was in the form of God, didn't count equality with God a thing to be grasped, but emptied himself, by taking the form of a servant, being born in the likeness of men. And being found in human form, he humbled himself by becoming obedient to the point of death, even death on a cross. (Philippians 2:5–8)

Reading this passage should strip us of any sense of entitlement. Jesus "emptied himself." Jesus took on "the form of a servant." The God of the universe washed his disciples' feet. He carried his own cross to his place of death! If anyone in the history of the world had a right to walk the streets of earth with a sense that he was owed something, it was Jesus because *he was*! Yet, he chose to walk humbly and peacefully. He was the most powerful person to ever walk earth. He created earth! Yet his life was characterized by meekness, power restrained. He never demanded the respect from people he was due. Why? Because he drew his strength and his significance from his relationship with the Father and not from men's opinions. He knew who he was because he knew what his Father thought of him.

What about you? What about me? Is our sense of self-worth derived from the opinions (real or perceived) of men or from our deep knowledge of who God says we are? Do we even know who God says we are? Let me give a hint, God says we are so valuable, that he was willing to lay down his life for us. God thinks we are so special. He left the wonderfulness of heaven to come and live in poverty on earth and face a criminal's death, so we could experience the heaven he knows through faith in him. Sounds like his opinion should be the only one that matters, right?

Put Your Behind in the Past and Forget about the Future

You gotta love the philosophers, Timon and Pumba, who made famous the quote, "Put your behind in the past." Sure we've all heard this and have head knowledge of this necessity, but do we actually live it? Dwelling on past hurts, hang-ups, failures, or losses will do nothing but damage our present and future effectiveness. We *must* let them go. No amount of worry and fretting about yesterday can change yesterday, but it certainly can negatively impact the present and future. Failures are simply opportunities to learn, so we can be better next time. Pain, hurt, and loss are opportunities to grow and get stronger.

Likewise, stressing about the future is unreasonable and leads to insecurity, irrational thought, and irrational behavior as well. Worry about the future is always a by-product of reliving negativity of the past. Jesus said, "How many of you by worrying has added a single hour to his life?" If we get all worked up about things that may never come to pass, how has this aided us, the potential situation, or any party involved? It only makes our present (and those around us!) miserable.

One of mine and my wife's favorite movies is the 2003 version of *The Italian Job* starring Mark Wahlberg, Charlize Theron, Jason Statham, Ed Norton, Donald Sutherland, Seth Green, Mos Def, and others. As the crew prepared for their heist of stealing gold bricks from a double-crosser, Donald Sutherland's character scolded not to use the word *fine* to describe how one is doing when asked, especially not prior to pulling a job. Why? Because he believed FINE is an acronym for: *F*reaked out, *I*nsecure, *N*eurotic, and *E*xcitable. He wanted his team to be ready, prepared, calm, confident, collected. If they were the other four words, chances were the job would go poorly because they would panic, forget their mark, lose faith in the plan, and rush past important steps.

The same is true in life, and Jesus knows that. He also knows that it's impossible to have a "peace that surpasses all understanding" without the one who is the creator of peace, namely, himself. Peace is only found in Christ. Self-actualization leads to deep feelings of inadequacy, with only superficial confidence. Self-help and other religions impose sets of rules and rituals that can leave the practitioner in a constant state of anxiousness wondering, "Did I do enough today?" Only Jesus says, "Come to me all who are weary and burdened, and I will give you rest." Only Christ took our place and accomplished all that needed to be accomplished so that we could be assured of peace on earth and eternal life simply through repentance, faith, and following him. We don't have to be F-I-N-E. Remember: *He is near.*

But How?

God is with us, but it can be difficult to remember and even harder to live with such an awareness. As a Christ follower, Jesus promised in Matthew 28:20 that he would always be with us as he said, "And behold, I am with you always, to the end of the age." He went away, but he sent back his Spirit to indwell the believer (John 14:17), and because of this, he proclaimed later in John 14:27, "Peace I leave with you, my peace I give you." So for the believer, we are assured of peace because the God of the universe who created all things and is never worried or surprised is living within us to give us his peace. For the nonbeliever, he or she can also have this assurance by placing faith in Christ and beginning a relationship with the Lord.

Yet we must admit that we do not always allow our thoughts and emotions to be controlled by his supernatural force living within. Unfortunately, part of our warring sin nature is to take back control of our psyche because we feel it is more responsible to worry and fret than to be at peace, filled with calm and joy. Jesus poses the rhetorical question in Matthew 6:27, "Who of you by worrying can add a single hour to his life?" to drive home the point that worrying is actually irresponsible and ridiculous. In fact, later in the passage, he actually commands us not to worry when he states, "Therefore, do not be anxious about tomorrow, for tomorrow will be anxious for itself. Sufficient for the day is its own trouble" (Matthew 6:34).

Though we know it is not in our new nature to worry and Christ actually commands us to not worry, why do we still do it, and how do we fight against it? I think that we can all agree that worrying is no fun. No one likes the feeling of anxiety. It's not pleasant. Let's explore some tips to help us avoid worry and live peacefully.

CHAPTER 4

Step 3

Pray

Do not be anxious about anything, but in everything with prayer and supplication and thanksgiving let your requests be made known to God.
—Philippians 4:6

My in-laws were at the 2020 ACC men's college basketball tournament. They called my wife and told her that everyone was just asked to vacate the arena. All games had been cancelled. Coronavirus cancel culture had started. For those who lived through this harrowing time, we remember how odd it felt to tug on a restaurant door only to find it was closed, to ride through town as one of the only cars on usually busy streets. It was easy to enter a state of anxiety, wondering if we would be able to work, eat, or find toilet paper! Watching the news or reading social media *did not* bring peace, did not help feelings of worry and dread. As the year plodded along, social unrest escalated in cities across our nation as the death toll continued to rise from the dreadful disease. Was our nation and culture imploding or becoming extinct? From where would hope and peace come? Many are still looking, but may I suggest the one who offers peace has already come, and he wants us to talk with him and listen to him.

Jesus promised in John 14:18, "I will not leave you as orphans: I will come to you." When we pray, we are asking with expectant hearts for the Lord to come to us, to hear our prayers, to answer our requests, to draw near to us as we draw near to him, for his will to be done, for our will to be aligned with his. We can be confident of all these things due to his promise above.

Earlier in John 14, Jesus states, "And I will do whatever you ask in my name, so that the Son may bring glory to the Father." It brings God joy to grant requests that we ask which are in sync with his plan. We know that from earlier discussed scripture that it is God's will for us to be at peace, so we can pray confidently for his peace and know that this prayer will be answered because it is done in Jesus' name. Any prayer that agrees with God's Word is guaranteed to be answered because Jesus was 100 percent in agreement with God's Word and Kingdom's agenda. He is the Word! He is God! So *pray*! "Pray continually" even as 1 Thessalonians 5:17 encourages.

Being in a continual state of prayer gives us the best chance to keep God's love, peace, and promises in the forefront of our minds and hearts and disallows the devil a good chance to gain a foothold in our hearts and minds. Remember that God is in us. So keep the conversation going. He desires that we speak to him. He desires that we listen to him.

I remember as a child, my dad asking me, "Can I get you anything?" Since I am, to a fault, self-sustaining and feel guilty being handed anything for fear of coming across as spoiled, my answer was always, "No." He'd continue, "Something to drink?" No. "Something to eat?" No. "A million dollars?" He'd press because he simply wanted to provide something for his son, to give a gift or necessity that would bring me joy would also bring him joy. I see this as how our Heavenly Father approaches prayer. He desires to give us what he desires to give us, and he wants us to recognize what he wants to give us and ask for it.

Ask Others to Pray for You

I recognize that sometimes, it is simply hard to pray. Those times when discouragement and doubt are so thick you simply want to lay down and veg out, it's difficult to think that your prayers would be effective or heard. When you feel that your faith is smaller than a mustard seed and you can't fathom the reason to pray because you feel it's a useless exercise, that is when it's a great idea to reach out and ask those you love and trust to pray for you.

Please know that I am speaking directly to myself here because it takes humility and trust to lay your deepest struggles, challenges, questions, thoughts, and fears before another human. If you are like me, you appreciate appearing that you've got it all together. Asking for prayer indicates that maybe, we don't. That's a hard pill to swallow. Pride is a tough nut to crack. And I certainly have a long way to go in laying it down. However, if the man who wrote two-thirds of the New Testament, Paul, can ask for prayer, why shouldn't we? He wrote in 1 Thessalonians 5:25, "Brothers, pray for us." Here he didn't mention specific requests like in other passages, but he was still humble enough to ask for prayer. Neither do we always have to mention exactly what we need prayer for, though I think we should have close-enough relationships with at least a few friends to do so, but we can at least ask, as Paul did, simply for prayer.

Just this week, a friend sent out a group text with only the words, "Fellas, unspoken prayer request." That was it. No details. Another friend, last week, sent a text that read, "Confidentially, I would really appreciate your prayers. I prefer to keep things close to myself, so I am only reaching out to you guys. Just pray for me to have peace with some things. Yes, I am going to leave it that general." That's it. No details on either. But you know what me and the other guys did? We prayed. And we continued to pray, never really knowing what we were praying for but having faith that God knew, so we prayed his peace to reign in these guys' lives and for his will to be done in each individual situation. I applaud these men for having the courage to reach out and ask for prayer. We can and should be willing to do the same.

Ask the Holy Spirit to Pray for You

The Bible says that "the Spirit himself intercedes for us with groaning too deep for words" (Romans 8:26). The Spirit of God, a third person of the Trinity, one of the three in One, goes before us and offers up prayers on our behalf even when we don't know what to pray, begs God's throne room for us in ways that we can't communicate, so our prayers are more effective and powerful. In the words of Steve Martin's character, Freddy, in *Dirty Rotten Scoundrels*, "*Wow!* All I can say is, 'Wow!'" What an incredible blessing that somehow, in a way that is foreign to our human minds to fully comprehend, God prays to himself for us!

A personal story of how this prayer helped me—I was on a plane headed overseas and entered into a tailspin of a panic attack envisioning our plane soon crashing into the polar ice caps. I could not get right mentally. I told myself to calm down. I got up and walked around, reminding myself that I had flown this route at least eight times, that statistics proved flying was so much more safe than driving, that surely God would not have called me to take this trip only for it to end in a fiery crash, leaving my wife and young kids disillusioned and alone. But after all the self-talk, I was still *freaking out*! Now we will discuss later in this book about the importance or replacing negative thoughts/words with positive thoughts/words because this activity is very helpful in giving peace and helping bring success, but in this instance, I needed something else. And no, I'm not referencing peyote. Though, perhaps...

As I sat in my coach seat, cramped and going crazy, the Lord clearly impressed upon me: "Pray to me. I'll pray for you." So I did. "Holy Spirit, please help me calm down. I can't get over these terrifying thoughts. Please, Holy Spirit, pray for me. Please help me to be at peace. I feel like I'm losing my mind. I can't seem to get over it. Please, Holy Spirit, bring me peace. Please calm my nerves."

After pleading for a few minutes, I truly felt back to myself. I was able to close my eyes and sleep. I awoke and felt normal. No more panic. What a breakthrough! And very needed for the remainder of my trip.

After landing safely at our initial destination, we transferred planes for another three-hour flight. Then we had a forty-five-minute window to lie down in a hotel bed before having to get back to the airport for our last leg. At the hotel, instead of crashing due to exhaustion (our travel time now approaching thirty-something hours), the crazy came back. "Well, you may have made it out of that flight alive, but you may not make this next one, and if you do, some bad stuff is definitely gonna happen on the trip. You may get arrested. Imprisoned. Your wife and kids will be alone and will never hear from you again. Oh, yeah, it's gonna be awful. You are doomed. In some ways, you are doomed. Just wait." Not exactly the rest I needed. However, thanks to the experience I had on the plane, as I funneled down the rabbit hole, I began to offer up my urgent prayers again, "Please, Holy Spirit, pray for me. Ask the Father to grant me peace to help overcome and replace these feelings and evil thoughts. Please. Please. Please."

I continued to pray for forty-five minutes, trying to combat the negativity. Thankfully by the time we had to board our next plane (after a six-hour layover because of weather delays), I was back to normal and that was great because our pilot took three attempts to land at our destination before finally pulling up and circling back to our origin due to high winds. People were getting sick, yelling in fear, crying. But not me. Praise God! Though the plane was getting blown about and those around me were suffering their own seventh circle of hell, I was as chill as if I were on a beach listening to Bob Marley. Thank you, Spirit, for praying for me and giving me peace that truly surpassed all understanding. Psalm 29:11b reads, "May the Lord bless his people with peace!" Yes. He can. He did for me. He will do the same for you. Just ask.

Ask Expectantly

We need to remember that when we ask, we must believe that our prayers will be answered. James 1:5–7 reads:

> If any of you lacks wisdom, let him ask God, who gives generously to all without reproach, and it will be given him. But let him ask in faith, without doubting, for the one who doubts is like a wave of the sea, tossed by the wind. For that

person must not suppose that he will receive anything from the Lord; he is a double-minded man, unstable in all his ways.

This passage is referring to asking for wisdom, but I think the same confident expectation would apply to asking the Lord for anything good. God wants us to come before him and expect that he will give us what definitely lines up with his will. We know it is in his will for us to love, to be joyful, to be at peace. It is his desire that we express and experience the fruit of the Spirit that we read about in Galatians 5, "love, joy, peace, patience, kindness, gentleness, faithfulness, and self-control." Therefore, it would be inappropriate to ask God for peace but still hold onto our fears.

Imagine you are dangling from a canyon cliff—nothing but air between you and a four-hundred-foot drop to a raging river below—tightly grasping two small branches. Your rescuer is securely on higher ground and has passed you a rope intended to pull you to safety. What do you have to do to grab the rope? You've got to open your hand, let go of one of those branches, and accept your lifeline. Accepting such a gift of the Spirit is similar. We have to be willing to let go of our worries, anxieties, and fears in order to have God's peace.

This reminds me of the first time I swam without my Styrofoam swim bubble strapped to my back when I was a young child. Dad took me to the diving board, unstrapped my swim bubble, and said, "You're gonna sink or swim." I realize that sounded a bit rough, but Dad knew I could do it. He had been watching me become a stronger swimmer all summer. He had seen my progress in our pool and at swimming lessons at our local YMCA. He believed in me before I believed in myself. Plus he was right there with me. Mom was a few feet away and could also come to my aid if need be. As I clung to him, unwilling to jump without my float, he asked a question he would ask multiple times again in my young life in various scenarios, "Son, have I ever done anything to hurt you?" My mind raced to find a "Yes" in order to save myself from the fearful event of swimming without my safety device, but all I could come up with was similar situations when he had made me try "scary" things that I ended up loving because they were so fun once the fear had been conquered. So I trepidatiously let go of his arms and allowed him to throw me in the deep end. And I swam. Never to go back to using a float again, joyously experiencing the freedom and fun of swimming unhindered by a Styrofoam bubble wrapped around my waist, no longer tethered to fear.

Our relationship with peace or worry is the same. God wants us to move through life with calm, not dread. He knows how good and freeing it is to live in confidence. He wants us to swim freely.

But God—

As I wrote the question above, "Son, have I ever done anything to hurt you?" I could hear your thoughts. "But God did [insert traumatic life event], and it hurt me. So how am I supposed to trust him again?" Good question. Let's explore.

Do we defy him in our thoughts, actions, and attitudes at times and bring godly discipline upon ourselves which he uses to bring us back to him? Yes. Does that bring pain and suffering at times? Yes. But situations like that are our own doing. God doesn't delight in our pain. God wants to bless us. Jesus said it himself in Luke 11:11, "What father among you, if his son asks for a fish, will instead of a fish give him a serpent; or if he asks for an egg, will give him a scorpion? If you then, who are evil, know how to give good gifts to your children, how much more will the heavenly Father give the Holy Spirit to those who ask Him!"

Conversely could God allow suffering or pain to prune us into what he wants us to be? Yes. Could that hurt emotionally or physically? Yes. John 15:1–2 is clear that God is the master gardener of our physical and spiritual lives. As Jesus teaches, "I am the true vine and my Father is the vinedresser. Every branch in me that does not bear fruit he takes away, and every branch that does bear fruit he prunes, that it may bear more fruit." So just as an attentive vinedresser cleans up the branches to allow better and bigger fruit for the benefit of the vine and the crop, we can expect our Father in heaven to do the same to our lives, and this may be less than pleasant and could seem harsh, but we must keep the reality in the forefront of our minds that God prunes for our good. Romans 8:28–29 is clear on this as it reads, "And we know that for those who love God, all things work together for good, for those who are called according to his purpose. For those whom he foreknew he also predestined to be conformed to the image of his Son, in order that he might be the firstborn among many brothers." These verses bring us assurance that God works *all* things together for the good of those who love him, those who have trusted him as Savior and are following him with their total lives. Furthermore, we can be certain that in is divine mind, knowing all from past to future, his plan has always been to make his children like Jesus—perfect and complete (eventually!).

We must remember that part of Christ's journey was suffering. So if God allowed suffering of his own Son, why would we be immune? Why would we want to be immune? James reminds us in chapter 1:2–4, "Count it all joy, my brothers, when you meet trials of various kinds, for you know that the testing of your faith produces steadfastness. And let steadfastness have its full effect, that you may be perfect and complete, lacking in nothing." Again, in these verses we can be comforted that trials are for our good, our maturation. Now just as running and running and running and running to prepare for a race may not be enjoyable, the satisfaction that comes from competing well makes the training worth it. Football players do not *love* training camp in late July, practicing two times per day in the blazing hot temperatures, but the suffering is worth the end result as they quickly get into shape and are prepared for the fast-approaching season.

We will do well to acknowledge that if we are truly following Christ, then difficulties, hardships, and trials are serving a purpose to make us better and more conformed to his image. This should give us joy and peace, as we are grateful to be counted worthy of God's time, attention, and effort.

Be Weak to Be Strong!

Paul was first a Jewish hitman tasked with killing Christians. After his conversion, he went on to evangelize most of the known world around the Mediterranean and wrote two-thirds of the New Testament. If anyone should have been protected from anxiety, stress, trouble, and persecution, we would expect it to be a guy like Paul. After all, he was living and breathing the gospel, traveling and sharing Christ's love. Shouldn't he be protected from difficulty, stress, and worry? He went from Christ enemy number one to Christ proclaimer number one. Yet in 2 Corinthians 11:23–28, he wrote:

> With far greater labors, far more imprisonments, with countless beatings, and often near death. Five times I received at the hands of the Jews the forty lashes less one. Three times I was beaten with rods. Once I was stoned. Three times I was shipwrecked; a night and a day I was adrift at sea; on frequent journeys, in danger from rivers, danger from robbers, danger from my own people, danger from Gentiles, danger in the city, danger in the wilderness, danger at sea, danger from false brothers, in toil and hardship, through many a sleepless night, in hunger and thirst, often without food, in cold and exposure. And, apart from other things, there is the daily pressure on me of my anxiety for all the churches.

Wow! When I read this, it makes me realize that many of the troubles we experience in our Western world, though awful at times, do not come close to all the difficulties Paul faced. And we must remember that he faced these hardships *because he was in God's will!* It was not as if Paul went through all these trials because of his disobedience and sin. He was seeking to please God and make his salvation known throughout the land, and that was exactly why he was faced with such calamity.

Jesus was crystal clear that such would occur. John 16:33 records Jesus stating, "In the world you will have tribulation." In John 10:10, Jesus is recorded as saying, "The thief comes only to kill, and steal and destroy." Jesus warned that the evil one, Satan, has only one mission: our destruction, anyone's destruction, but more so the destruction of those who seek to serve Christ. Later in the New Testament in 1 Peter 5:8, we read, "Be sober minded; be watchful. Your adversary the devil prowls around like a roaring lion, seeking someone to devour."

Considering such scripture and Paul's account of tribulations, I can sense that you may be thinking, "Hey, man, I thought this book was supposed to help give me victory over panic and lead me to peace, but this is only making me freak out all the more! God telling us that the devil is out there looking to devour me! Jesus promising that Satan is trying to kill me! Come on, man!"

I concede to such thoughts, but let's not forget to evaluate the totality of scripture. In other words, *let's get to the good stuff!*

The fullness of John 16:33, reads, "I have said these things to you, that in me you may have peace. In the world you will have tribulation. But take heart; I have overcome the world." Oh yeah! Where does our peace come from? Success? Health? Politicians? Government? Money? Fame? Fortune? No! We have peace *in Jesus*! Who has overcome the world? A President? A Senator? A business tycoon? An athlete? A scientist? No! Jesus has overcome the world! Only Jesus! He is the king of glory, and in him alone we can have peace! If, however, one is not in Christ—that is, one has not placed his faith in Christ, not believing and accepting he is God and his gift of forgiveness through his death, burial, and resurrection—then one has no hope for true peace.

In John 10, after Jesus had warned against Satan, he gave us words of comfort and hope when he said, "I came that they may have life and have it abundantly." He brought to our attention that he was 180 degrees diametrically opposed to the plotting of Satan. He reminds us that he is not a distant deity in the sky looking to smite us with lightning bolts and brimstone. He is a loving and gentle God desiring that we have abundant life.

And what about the second half of the verse in 1 Peter 5 about the roaring lion? The Bible reminds us to "resist him, firm in your faith, knowing that the same kinds of suffering are being experienced by your brotherhood throughout the world." Isn't it comforting to know that you have the power to resist, and that, you are not in the fight alone?

This leads me to think of personal experience of sports training. During preseason training, my coaches would put us through misery to get us in shape for the approaching season. We would be pushed past points that we may have been unable to achieve alone because we were suffering as a team. Because we were unified in our trials—running, lifting, etc.—we were able to achieve more individually and as a team.

God reminds us that we are not on a hill alone. We have fellow sojourners through the difficulties of life. Yet it may be up to us to connect with them in person or via technology. There is peace and strength in numbers. Even in the movies, the cop who *never has a partner* ends up needing a partner and appreciating the relationship by the end of the story. We need each other.

Romans 16:20 goes on to remind us that "the God of peace will soon crush Satan under your feet." Our job is to resist. God will do the crushing of that roaring lion! Doesn't that give you a sense of relief and victory? We resist with our brothers and sisters, and God comes in and does the cleanup! It's like when a group of soldiers is barely holding the line, they are being overrun, but they are able to resist just long enough to call in an air strike which totally eradicates the enemy position. Hold on! God is coming! Be comforted that the God of Peace is fighting for you.

I recognize that many of us don't feel we have the power and strength sufficient to even hold the line during times of stress, panic, and chaos. So please consider the following and be encouraged.

Paul writes in 2 Corinthians 12:9, "But he said to me, 'My grace is sufficient for you, for my power is made perfect in weakness.' Therefore, I will boast all he more gladly of my weakness so that the power of Christ may rest upon me." Paul noted prior in this same passage how he had a "thorn in the flesh, a messenger from Satan to harass me." No one is certain exactly what the thorn was, but most likely, it was some type of affliction, mental wound, insecurity, an annoying person maybe. Whatever it was, it was really unpleasant and was wearing him out. He notes that he "pleaded with the Lord" to remove it, but rather than removing the thorn, God encouraged him to be strong through the affliction, not with his own power and might but rather with the power and might of Christ working in and through him.

This can encourage us too. God's power is available to us through the indwelling of the Holy Spirit that lives within Christians. Romans 15:13 fortifies us with the words, "May the God of hope fill you with all joy and peace in believing, so that by the power of the Holy Spirit you may abound in hope." Though God has given each of us incredible capacities to be self-reliant, resilient, tough, and strong, ultimately in the Christian walk, it is the power of God's Holy Spirit that gives us the most fortification to endure and thrive. This is why we should boast in our weakness, so we can be strong in the Lord's mighty power.

In my previous book, *Thy Will Be Done?*, I recount the story and lessons learned as my wife and I walked through infertility issues, the blessing of a triplet pregnancy, and the struggles for our daughters (and us) due to preterm delivery. In one chapter near the end of the book, I wrote about the time my wife and I were essentially scolded for being too optimistic by one of the neonatal doctors and the hospital chaplain. They sat us down and admonished us for having a positive outlook and holding out hope that our daughter, Sophia, had any chance of survival. Though quite frustrated at the nature of the discussion, we gently explained to the doctor and the chaplain that we were fully aware of her bleak outlook, but since she was, in fact, still alive and since each day is a day to hope in our all-powerful God, we would not choose to live with an outlook and attitude of certain doom and gloom. While we still lived and she still lived, we would remain positive and hold out hope for her total earthly healing. This choice allowed us to wake each day and put one foot in front of the other even though each day could be her last.

I'd like to report that she turned the corner and was healed, but she wasn't. I'd also like to report that after our loss of the girls, I remained fully confident and steadfast in my positivity and peace, but I didn't. It took me years to accept Romans 8:28, and I'd be totally lying if I said each day it wasn't a battle in my mind and heart to truly believe that "all things work together for good for those who are called according to his purpose."

My faith is not perfected. I doubt yours is either. That is why we must make a daily choice to believe and trust that God is for us. And if he is for us, "then who can be against us?"

CHAPTER 5

Step 4

Accept God's Peace vs. the World's Peace

Jesus said, "Peace I leave with you; my peace I give to you. Not as the world gives do I give to you. Let not your heart be troubled, neither let them be afraid."
—John 14:27

In the above passage, Jesus is addressing his most closely trusted disciples and is encouraging them with the truth that he would grant them supernatural peace that could protect them from anxiety and fear. His time on earth was nearing the end, and it would end tragically and violently. He knew what he was to soon endure and how his quick capture, trial, and execution had the potential to wreck his disciples' faith and confidence, so he spoke preemptively to encourage them. He specifically noted that he does not give "as the world gives," indicating that his peace would be complete, whole, and not dependent on circumstance.

We have worldly peace when our bank account is greater than sufficient. We have worldly peace when our health is perfect. We have worldly peace when our career is secure and business is thriving. However, we can have the peace of Jesus when any of those circumstances crumbles. He knew his disciples would be scattered, persecuted, and hated, so he had to bolster their confidence, reminding them that his peace would usurp the worldly struggles they would soon face. If we are in Christ, this same peace is available to us. Jesus did not offer his peace to everyone, only to those who were following him closely. What's the takeaway? Knowing Jesus as Savior leads to true and lasting peace. If we don't know him, we simply cannot have his peace upon our lives. Good news though, he is still calling to those who haven't trusted him with their lives and souls. He still desires to "draw men (and women) unto" himself. So his peace is available. His peace is transcendent. His peace is otherworldly. His peace is supernatural and complete.

"But I Know Jesus as Savior, and I'm Still Overcome with Worry."

Statements or thoughts like the header above are certainly common, especially this day and time. And they can lead to a person feeling guilty and even more upset for committing the sin of worry. When we are worried about worrying, we are headed down a quick vortex of despair. But it doesn't have to be that way. Jesus didn't say, "Do not be anxious," in Matthew 6 because he was trying to give us a command to keep. Rather he was reminding us that we don't have to worry because God is in control. We are not. What good does it do to worry anyway?

Jesus stated, "And which of you by being anxious can add a single hour to his span of life?" (Matthew 6:27), essentially asking us to really consider the frivolity of worry. We are not helping the situation by being overly concerned about it. Prayer, planning, and action? Sure. These are all good, active pursuits proving that we believe God is in control and he has given us the capacity to act through his guidance and power. But sitting around wringing our hands is no way to live. It's not honoring to God and not helpful for us. Then, at the end of this passage in Matthew, Jesus boiled down his teaching to the wisdom for us to "seek first the kingdom of God and his righteousness, and all these things will be added to you. Therefore, do not be anxious about tomorrow, for tomorrow will be anxious for itself. Sufficient for the day is its own trouble" (Matthew 6:33–34).

One of the gazillion awesome things about Jesus is that he doesn't just give us instructions and then leave us to fend for ourselves, wondering how we will ever have the capacity to carry them out. Later in the book Matthew records Jesus encouraging us when he writes, "I will never leave you nor forsake you" (28:20). *Never.* He is with us always. We are *never* alone. He is everywhere, but he is right here with us at the same time. He is Lord of all creation and also Lord of our hearts.

John 14:16–17 reads, "And I will ask the Father, and he will give you another Helper, to be with you forever, even the Spirit of truth, whom the world cannot receive, because it neither sees him nor knows him. You know him for he dwells with you and will be in you." Jesus is with us and in us. He is Lord of all cares and concerns we may have. He is Lord of all situations that may arise. Because he is King and he is with us, we can proceed through life at peace. We can be like my youngest son, Tyson, and cover our fears with the grace and power of God's abiding presence. During a recent tornado warning, when we were all huddled in an inner room of our home during the middle of the night, he wanted to be held, and he also wanted to have his blanket covering his head because he said he was "hiding from the thunder." We must keep the reality cognitively and emotionally present before us that we are under the cover of God's mighty hand no matter what storm we are facing or could face in the future. And remember that storms we could face in the future are not storms at all and may never spin into one in the first place, so we should not give credence to a negative idea and allow it to have any control over our emotions or attitudes. Remember: Put your behind in the past, and don't project it into the future!

To recap, in this section we have journeyed through how we can have confidence in Paul's instructions from Philippians 4:6–7 by consciously eliminating worry, offering up our concerns to God, and trusting in his outcome. I'll write his words again: "Do not be anxious about anything, but in everything by prayer and supplication with thanksgiving let your request be made known to God. And the peace of God, which surpasses all understanding, will guard your hearts and your minds in Christ Jesus."

CHAPTER 6

Step 5

Replace Bad with Good

> *Finally brothers, whatever is true, whatever is honorable, whatever is just, water is pure, whatever is lovely, whatever is commendable, if there is any excellence, if there is anything worthy of praise, think about these things.*
> —Philippians 4:8

In the previous chapters, we explored how God's peace can transform and fill us by us simply gratefully surrendering to the realization that he is in control, loves us, and has great plans for us. Let's move now to our active part of moving from panic to peace.

As he nears the end of the discussion on perfect peace, Paul gives a list of attributes that should fill our minds. In essence, he is instructing us to dwell on good things. To do this, we must make the conscientious choice to replace negative thoughts and emotions with positive ones. This is an active, thoughtful process. It is a daily discipline. Negative, painful, fearful, lustful, worrisome, angry, limiting thoughts will try to rule our minds and hearts, but we must remember that as much as the Lord allows, we are in control of our minds, and we, therefore, have the capacity to drive out, ignore, or change the evil to good.

Life and power are in the written and spoken word. Otherwise, we would not have a book, the Bible, that is a *written* record of God's spoken words! Consider John 1:1–2, *"In the beginning was the Word, and the Word was with God, and the Word was God. He was in the beginning with God."* This passage, opening the gospel of John, clearly indicates that Christ is the totality of the *Word* of God. What did God do with his Word? He created the universe. He gave knowledge of himself to his creation. He offered his love. He presented warnings and the path of repentance. He made the way of salvation through his Word, Jesus Christ. Since God's words are so powerful and we were made in his image, we must be aware that our words have the ability to create and heal—or destroy. Proverbs 18:21 reminds us of this truth as it reads, *"Death and life are in the power of the tongue."* So we have a very real responsibility to be active in insuring our minds and mouths are filled with positive, affirming, life-giving thoughts and words. As Jesus said, "Out of the overflow of the heart, the mouth speaks."

As we explore this ever-important discipline of replacing negative with positive, we should realize this is not something new to us. If someone is going on a diet, will they not replace bad food with good food? If a person is deciding to get physically fit, will he not replace couch sitting with exercise? We understand the necessity to make changes and replacements in our physical life. Our mental life is no different. I suppose I had always been aware of God's instruction on this through Paul's writing, but it really did not sink in until January of 2020, as I was sitting in a massage chair next to my friend and older brother in the Lord as we decompressed from a week of heavy activity by indulging in foot massages. We were in a small city in Asia where our team had been coaching basketball clinics all week, and my friend and I were rehashing a devotion I had shared a day or two to prior with our coaches. The Lord had impressed upon me to lead a discussion on John 10. In this passage, Jesus is sharing how his sheep know his voice. It is worth including the entire passage.

"Truly, Truly, I say to you, he who does not enter the sheepfold by the door but climbs in by

another way, the man is a thief and a robber. But he who enters by the door is the shepherd of the sheep. To him the gatekeeper opens. The sheep hear his voice, and he calls his own sheep by name and leads them out. When he has brought out all his own, he goes before them, and the sheep follow him, for they know his voice. A stranger they will not follow, but they will flee from him, for they do not know the voice of strangers." This figure of speech Jesus used with them, but they did not understand what he was saying to them. So Jesus said to them, "Truly, truly I say to you, I am the door of the sheep. All who came before me are thieves and robbers, but the sheep did not listen to them. I am the door. If anyone enters by me, he will be saved and will go in and out and find pasture. The thief comes to steal, and kill and destroy. I came that they may have life and have it abundantly. I am the good shepherd. The good shepherd lays down his life for the sheep." (John 10:1–11)

I think the Lord gave me this passage to share in our devotion because his voice had been very clear to me through an attempt by the thief to disguise himself as the true voice over that past year. For nearly one year prior to my conversation described above, I had been bombarded by thoughts and feelings of worthlessness, despair, fear, impending doom, dread, and an internal rationalization that the world would be better off without me. I'm not sure what the trigger was—perhaps the loss of my stepdad a few months prior, perhaps an infection that caused possible brain swelling (as a neurologist I consulted had suggested), or perhaps just the devil attacking my psyche. All I know now is that I was not right mentally or spiritually for many months, and my wife and kids can attest. But *praise God* because he rescued me from the darkness by his goodness and by the light of his Word.

Jesus's affirming words broke through and brought me out of the abysmal pattern of thinking. It's like literally one day, the clouds broke, and I could see clearly again. I had an awareness, as I do now, that I had been enshrouded by darkness and lies for months. Now, mind you, during this time of what I feel was spiritual oppression and warfare, when the enemy was trying to take me out physically and mentally, I was spending time with the Lord daily—praying, reading the Word, journaling. I was leading discipleship groups. I was in an accountability relationship. I was avoiding sin. There was no hidden sin. My marriage was pure. My business was thriving. I was working out five to six days per week. Meaning, there was no *reason* for the darkness that I can figure. It's not like I was living a lie, eating ice cream and chips all day, laying around the house watching daytime television, floundering professionally, or in a midlife crisis. I was doing all the things that I had always done, but I was in a dark hole for months, and I did not even know I was in the hole. That being said, I think deeper than the darkness was the truth of Jesus and his Word rooted in my heart that was reminding me of my worth in him—that I had value and purpose, that my wife and kids would *not* be better off without me (maybe that's why I watched *It's a Wonderful Life* three times the prior Christmas! Ha!), and that God has a purpose and plan for my life and that plan was for good and not for harm! Otherwise, why would he have created me?!

It comes back to truth. Truth is the opposite of lies. Jesus only speaks truth, and thanks be to his Holy Spirit living in me, I was able to wade through the lies to hear the truth. Jesus mentions that the sheep "follow him, for they know his voice." Can you differentiate the voice of truth verses the voice of lies? This is crucial in order to have a life of peace. Had I not been able to tell the difference during that period of attempted theft of my heart and mind, things would have turned out very differently, very poorly. I am so thankful that God saw fit to save me years ago from my sin, placed his Spirit within me, and placed a desire in me to know him and read his Word, so I'd have the spiritual wisdom by his grace to see through the lies and come back to the light and truth.

However, my friend, if you do not have a personal relationship with Christ, if his Holy Spirit does not indwell you, then how are you going to be able to tell the difference between truth and lies? It's impossible. The Bible gives us a warning that the evil one goes about disguising as an angel of light (2 Corinthians 11:14). Therefore, if we do not have discernment given by God's Holy Spirit, we are hopeless to be able to stand against his schemes. And we must remember, as Jesus proclaimed in the passage above, the thief, Satan, comes to "steal, kill, and destroy." His words to you may seem right at the time, but they are not. They only have your spiritual, personal, and eternal destruction in mind. He is your worst enemy. He wants to take you out, so you can suffer for eternity like he will suffer for eternity because of his rebellion against the God who made him.

I recognize that some reading this book may be turned off since I'm writing about spiritual warfare and seemingly demanding that being a follower of Christ is the only hope of having a life of peace, not panic, but I urge you to hear me out and not quit reading. Can we fill our lives and minds with positive practices and mantras that have the capacity to usher in peace amid chaos? Are there tenets of self-help, other religions, meditation, Oprah or Tony Robbins that offer peace and contentment to our hearts and minds? Yes. I agree there are. Have some of you tried Christianity only to find that it didn't work for you? Probably so. But may I suggest a few things in regard to these questions.

Trying Christianity is totally different than following Christ. Jesus did not ask us to try and follow his teaching. He asked us to lay our lives down at his feet and give him our total devotion because he gave his total life for us on the cross. True Christianity is total submission to the God who loves us through turning from ourself (admitting that we can't be good enough to earn his favor) and turning to him for salvation. But salvation from what? Salvation from eternal judgment by God for not making him our king. So people who tried Christianity only to abandon it never really owned it to be able to abandon it. One can try other religions because they are *all* centered around our ability to do enough (of whatever they ask) and avoid enough (of whatever they ask) in order to earn favor. If one finds a flavor of religion that he feels he can balance the "do this/don't do that" in his perceived favor, then there could be a sense of peace that ensues.

"Yeah, I'm really good at making my vows, burning my incense, praying my prayers, and avoiding X, Y, Z, so I'm good with my god. He/She will allow me nirvana in the afterlife and material blessings until then." However, deep down, because there will always be that tension of "Did I really do enough?" this person is still at odds, spiritually and emotionally. This person will still be lacking true peace, whether he admits it or not.

It has been said that man's greatest motivations are pain avoidance and pleasure seeking, and we are the most motivated to avoid pain over indulging in pleasure. This is why we see many heart attack victims stop eating junk and begin working out. The pleasure of eating cheeseburgers and drinking milk shakes while living a sedentary life is not as great a motivator as avoiding another heart attack or having a stroke that may leave you in awful physical shape or dead. Spiritually we all want to avoid eternal punishment by whatever god/God we believe in, or at the very least, we want to feel certainty that when this life is over, we know what awaits us. Thus, eventually, most of us will seek to make ourselves right before our Creator before it's too late, primarily to avoid the pain of uncertainty or potential eternal punishment but also in order to enjoy the benefits of a right relationship with our deity as we travel through life.

So back to my original point in this section, without a saving true faith in Christ, there will be no real peace because only Jesus states, "I am *the* way, *the* truth, and *the* life." He makes no allowance that there are any other ways of eternal peace and salvation from damnation. Only Jesus. God's word reminds us that "for by grace you have been saved, through faith. And this is not your own doing; it is the gift of God, not a result of works, so that no one may boast" (Ephesians 2:8–9). There is absolutely nothing we can do to earn his favor. We just have to admit that we know our good will never outweigh our bad, that Jesus took the punishment we deserved, and accept God's free gift of salvation through faith in these truths. This denial of self-salvation (following other religious paths, good outweighing bad) and submission to the God who loves you so much will usher in lasting and true peace. I know personally.

Moving Past Relationships to Personal Practice

The Bible passage at the top of this chapter lays out some practical steps to help us as we journey toward lasting peace. Yes, I realize that I just spent several paragraphs diagramming how peace comes through a relationship with Christ, not through practicing a religion. While this is true, as we follow Him, there are tenets we should include in our lives that go beyond simply believing his truth. Just as we would not enter a dating relationship or get married and then refuse to go on dates, call, text, purchase birthday or Christmas presents, etc. and expect a successful relationship, neither should we live by the mantra: "Yeah, I follow Jesus, but I don't really do anything he says." That being established, let's dive deeper into the above word.

Honorable

If something or someone is honorable, it is held in high regard. It is a thought, item, or person that would be considered worthy of respect and good standing. If our minds are cluttered with inappropriate, negative, hurtful, selfish thoughts, then we will spiral into fear, dread, and even shame. Comparing ourselves to others to the point of jealousy or bitterness is not honorable thinking. Lustful thoughts (sexual or financial) does not evoke a sense of honor. However, the virtues of love, kindness, joy, purity, and selflessness, among others (see Galatians 5:22–23) are laden with honor. They are thoughts worthy of being brought to light and exposed. They put others first and build up rather than tear down. We must train our minds to think honorably.

Just

What is justice? The definition of *just* is "based on or behaving according to what is right, good, or fair." Easy to define with a dictionary but difficult to define in reality. What is right, good, or fair, and who has the ability to establish such benchmarks? Is it the government? Is it the media? Is it the latest movement? If so, from where do they derive their authority and their guidelines to proclaim their form of justice? These questions matter greatly because if we are to fill our minds with just thoughts, but our definition of justice is skewed, then we could be filling our minds with the wrong thoughts, just as if our understanding of truth is actually not true, we end up thinking the wrong things.

May I suggest that our only source for a true portrait of justice comes from God and the Bible. The Word is clear that God is the only purely holy and righteous one (see Romans 3:23). The Bible is also clear that God will judge all who have sinned against him. That means everyone in all creation (see Hebrews 9:27, Romans 6:23a). Thankfully, God's Word is also clear that God satisfied his wrath against the sin of humanity by placing his punishment on Jesus instead, thereby justly satisfying his wrath and offering forgiveness for all who believe (see Romans 3:23, 6:23b, 10:9–10; Ephesians 2:8–10). So what does this mean? How do we take this knowledge to mold our thoughts to those of justice?

First, we realize there is an established order of right and wrong, of good and fair, and that this established order is set by the only God in heaven, the God of the Bible. Secondly, we live with extreme gratitude that God did not deny his attribute of justice to offer forgiveness to us, but that, he, instead, fulfilled his justice by allowing himself to be sacrificed on the cross in our place. What a sense of joy and thankfulness we can have each day as we remind ourselves of God's love and forgiveness as we consider his justice! Because of Christ, we can be right with God! What a sense of peace this can bring knowing our sins are forgiven and our eternity is secure! Let us not look to the justice of sinful man which can sway with the winds of change. Let us look, instead, to the justice of the righteous God that is set for eternity so we can be at peace.

Pure

Nothing is purer than God, so we dwell on him. Is this suggesting that we all enter monasteries and spend our lives chanting, praying, and reading the Scripture? *No.* Why? Because that would take us out of the world that God wants us to impact. But it does mean that our minds are to be stayed on thoughts that are clean, whole, and undefiled. This repetition of thought, being in the same vein as honorable, is certainly placed in this passage for a purpose. The purity of our thought matters immensely for our personal peace. What are the fruits of lust, envy, anger, jealousy, rage? All *bad*! Conversely what are the fruits of a man being thoughtful of only his wife and no other woman, his mind stayed on the well-being of his children, his attention captured by bringing honor to God, his mind focused only on the symbiotic good of his business and coworkers, not being selfish for personal gain, happy for friends' promotions or success, excited for a neighbor's new car? All *good*!

This reminds me of the movie from 2019 in which Tom Hanks depicted Mr. Rogers. What a fabulous movie, in my opinion, and I highly recommend it! The protagonist of the story was a reporter who was depicted as a very jaded journalist with a dysfunctional past and present. He was tasked to simply interview Fred Rogers for a magazine piece. The journalist makes it his goal to expose Mr. Rogers as a fake—presupposing that no one can be as pure and kind and gentle as Mr. Rogers appears. Yet he fails miserably at his expose as he learns (through a developed relationship) that Mr. Rogers is actually just as advertised. His motives and actions were truly pure, and he wanted nothing but the best for people. Mr. Rogers thought pure, and his life was a reflection of his thoughts—peaceful and pure. Yours can be too.

Lovely, Commendable, Admirable, Excellent, Praiseworthy

The last few words in this Philippians passage are all very similar in nature and convey similar commands in regard to our thought life. We are to be certain to fill our minds with ideas, memories, or projections of people, places, attributes, character traits, or virtues that evoke God—honoring pure joy and delight. What may some examples be?

First, we start with the Sunday school answer: Jesus. Not trying to be cliché, but it is actually true. Dwelling on the perfect Lamb of God, the author and perfecter of our faith, our rock, our redeemer, the bright morning star, the King of Kings and Lord of Lords, the lover of our souls can't help but bring us peace and encouragement.

Brennan Manning in his book, *The Furious Longing of God*, writes of how taking several minutes per day to sit quietly, palms up (signifying surrender), repeating the phrase in prayer to the Lord, "Abba, I'm yours," has made a tremendous difference in his life and the lives of many others who have practiced this holy meditation, reminding them that they are the child of the true, loving King. I mean, come on! The King of Glory chose to redeem us through his own blood so we could be a part of his eternal reigning family! If that thought doesn't get you pumped up and filled with gratitude, then I don't know what will. Understanding this truth brings an eternal and abiding joy that cannot be shaken.

Coming out of the ethereal, some worldly examples of great thoughts to push out the negative would be anything that is good and wholesome (i.e. not sinful) that fills your mind and heart with warm feelings such as a child's laugh or smile, your favorite vacation spot, your best view of a sunrise or sunset, sunny mornings, summer nights, rainy days, frost-covered mornings near Christmas, your most memorable vista, great memories, friends, coffee, tea, food, love, peace, conversation, laughter, jokes, funny stories, your favorite movie, the list could go on. The point is, by filling our minds with good, we push out the bad. By filling our minds with thoughts that bring joy and peace, we shove out dread and worry. This encourages us and honors God.

What about thoughts that are praiseworthy? What could this phrase mean, and how could it apply? What qualities about God, yourself, or others would you consider to be worthy of praise? How about love, forgiveness, selflessness, valor, bravery, courage, humility, patience, kindness, gentleness, self-control, peace, joy, gratefulness, faithfulness, goodness? Such character traits are truly worthy of praise. Running words such as these through our minds throughout the day keeps negative words, thoughts, and emotions at bay. Just as darkness cannot exist in the presence of even the smallest light, so worry, fear, and dread cannot coexist in the presence of peace and joy. But we must *work* to keep the good before us and in us, just as a camper must *work* to keep his embers burning all night lest the cold, darkness, and wolf creep into the camp. It is a daily decision, a conscientious choice to dwell on lovely, commendable, excellent, admirable, and praiseworthy thoughts, attitudes, and attributes. As an athlete cannot miss days of workouts or practice for fear of being taken over by his opponent, neither can we miss minutes or hours of being emotionally and spiritually on guard and in control, or we run the risk of being taken captive by darkness.

"But it's hard!" you say.

Yeah. I know. But everything worthwhile is usually hard. That doesn't make working toward the goal any less worthy or achievable. However, I think we do need some practical tools to help us in this daily battle. Here are a few:

1. Spend daily time in prayer and reading and reflecting on the Bible. I suggest starting your day with this time to get your mind set and focused for the day.
2. Consider making scripture memorization cards that you carry with you, or write scripture you'd like to memorize on the notes in your phone, so when you have a few extra minutes, instead of falling into the trap of comparing yourself to the world on social media or filling your mind with doomsday salesmen by scanning news sites, put the Word in your brain instead!
3. Practice the meditation mentioned above suggested by Brennan Manning. Sit quietly, palms up, eyes closed in prayer to God repeating, "Abba, I'm yours."
4. Be in a constant state of prayer. First Thessalonians 5:17 encourages us to "Pray continually." If our minds are continually focused on an internal dialogue with God, we have a much greater chance of our minds staying filled with good thoughts, peaceful thoughts.
5. Read encouraging books.

6. Dwell on the good qualities you see in people you love, admire, and respect and make the effort to be around them more. Charlie "Tremendous" Jones said, "You will be the same person in five years as you are today except for the people you meet and the books you read."
7. Be a good-finder in others and in circumstances. During your day, look for reasons to praise others. Find reasons to be thankful in any and every situation. My daughter, Avery, is so good at this. Even when she gets under some sort of restriction for disobedience to a family rule, she will turn it around to the positive as in, "I guess it's good I got my iPad taken away for two weeks. That means I'll read and practice guitar more."
8. If you can't find anything excellent or praiseworthy, look harder!
9. Consider a daily "Excellent and Praiseworthy/Grateful" journal. Take one minute each morning and/or evening to write the top three people, experiences, blessings of your day or in regard to the coming day.

Hopefully these truths and suggestions for replacing negative with positive will help. Actually I'm certain they will if we follow them. Just like a gym membership does not help us stay in shape unless we actually go there and use the equipment, unless we utilize these tools, we are at risk of continuing to allow the world's negativity to dominate our thoughts and hearts. Let's not do that. Let's attack negativity with positivity and overcome evil with good.

CHAPTER 7

Step 6

Stop the Comparison Game

> *You shall not covet your neighbor's house; you shall not covet your neighbor's wife, or his male servant, or his female servant, or his ox, or his donkey, or anything that is your neighbor's.*
> —Exodus 20:17

"Look at their amazing vacation photos! They must make a killing to be able to travel as much as they do. Here I am trying to scratch out enough extra cash to take the kids to the fair when it comes to town, and those jokers are in Bora Bora!"

"Look how beautiful she is. I'll never be able to wear something like that. I wish I could, but all my clothes have to be baggy to cover up this frumpy figure I've got. Why couldn't I be blessed with a beautiful face and flawless body? She's gotta be taking diet pills and touching up those photos!"

"How is it that their kids are so well behaved and have such great manners and mine are running around like a couple of drunk monkeys?! Why can't I get my kids to listen and respect me like they do theirs?!"

"Look at their house and those cars! They have more money in cars than my house is even worth! Why didn't I do whatever they do for a profession?!"

"Look at that photo of those two. They are truly the perfect couple. Always smiling. Always have it together. Why can't my marriage be perfect like theirs? I bet they never fight and find time to connect emotionally and physically every night. We are lucky to have time to argue for five minutes before falling asleep, exhausted at the end of each day."

If you're like most people, you have had similar thoughts to the ones posted above at some time in your recent past. Maybe even today! Here's how it went—You opened up your favorite social media app, scrolled down the page, and the barrage of comparative thoughts flooded your mind. Instead of feeling encouraged and relaxed from seeing your friends and family having fun, looking good, and enjoying life, you became discouraged and stressed wondering how their lives were so good and yours was so mediocre. Then you probably threw down your phone and yelled at somebody. *Ha!* Am I right?!

Maybe there really was something to God's warning to not be jealous. He knew that jealousy—coveting what our neighbors had—would not only affect our relationship with him and them, but it would also poison our souls, making us bitter and sour. Envy leads to stress and anger. Therefore, we must guard our hearts against this state. Not only so, but it also leads to us being mad at God. "God, why didn't you give me a body or face like hers/his? God, why do I have such a low-paying dead-end job? God, why can't I take my entire family to that Caribbean all-inclusive resort each year? God, why is my house falling in, and they live in a mansion? God, why can't I seem to lose weight, and she looks like a supermodel?"

In reality, when we step back and consider each of the above jealous complaints, many of them may not have anything to do with God's blessing or curse but rather are dependent on our effort. It's just so much easier to blame someone for our perceived lack of success than it is to own up to the fact that we are the ones to blame. A giant leap in the opportunity to live at peace is accepting personal responsibility. We can experience a great measure of calm by walking according to the goals and guidelines we set for ourselves. One author stated that true success is the "progressive realization of a worthy ideal." In other words, making consistent effort to achieve a dream goal gives us satisfaction, and we will be at peace knowing we are achieving consistent marks of progress. Of course this means that we need to have the fortitude to actually follow through with striving to achieve our goals and plans. If we simply push off goals as dreams that we never make steps toward achieving, then we can become stuck in the quagmire of self-doubt and pity. We must truly progressively realize the dream, take small steps daily, become better every day, and stop comparing our lives to everyone else's. Enjoy our journey.

Remember Whose You Are

When we stop comparing ourselves to others and allow who we are (whole, completely in Christ, empowered by his Holy Spirit, forgiven, redeemed) to be sufficient, then our outlook and attitude can be one of peace. Our self-worth should be found solely in Christ alone and who he says we are. And who does he say we are? He says we are born with inherent worth and value (Jeremiah 29). He says we are worth dying for (John 3:16). He says we are heirs of his Kingdom (Romans 8:17).

I am not suggesting that we should stop striving to improve or become proud, fat, and happy, resting on our laurels thinking, "I'm a child of the King. Why do I need to do anything else in this world?" To the contrary, because we (followers of Christ) have been given such great love and assurance, this should push us to be our best, realizing our worth is not based on our worldly-measured performance but in our relationship with Jesus. He loves us, period. And out of that understanding and realization, we happily and healthily strive for greatness here on earth to please him and point others to him. We read a confirmation of this in 1 Corinthians 10:31, "So whether you eat or drink or whatever you do, do it all for the glory of God." Living with the understanding that our worth is rooted in Christ's opinion of us (Remember: It's great!) and working consistently to improve daily in order to please our King and give him glory gives us a sense of hope, purpose, and joy. We can also be certain that everything we face in this life is ordained by God and for our good and his glory.

Romans 8:28 reminds us, "And we know that for those who love God all things work together for good, for those who are called according to his purpose." The question is: Do you love God? Do you have a true relationship with him based on the truth of the Scripture? Have you turned from the idea that you can be good enough to earn God's favor and asked him to be your Savior and King? Is your life rooted in Christ? If not, at some deeper level, though you may employ all the above peace-giving techniques, you will never truly be at rest—spiritually, mentally, emotionally. Even the most devout, apparently peaceful Buddhist monk living in a temple high in the Himalayas is admittedly constantly searching for truth. Christ is truth. Know him, and know peace.

SET UP YOUR BEACH CHAIR

As we wind down this little book that was set in motion by three little birds and you are preparing your spot in the sand on your journey from panic to peace, please accept this last bit of encouragement.

It is imperative to abide in the reality, attitudes, outlooks, and actions mentioned in God's word and in this text. The Word reminds us to "Therefore, take up the whole armor of God" (Ephesians 6:13), and we must do this daily because as Jesus said in his command to not worry, "Sufficient for the day is its own trouble" (Matthew 6:34). Jesus was reminding us that each day brings its own worries, so we must be ready to face each day with the weapons he gives us to fight against such potential anxiety-producing circumstances, weapons like the six small steps we've discussed: Rejoice, Be Gentle, Pray, Accept God's Peace, Replace Bad with Good, and Stop the Comparison Game. He didn't just remind us of this and give a proverbial pat on the back and send us on our way. His existence was to "guide our feet into the path of peace" (Luke 1:79). Be encouraged that he is with you (or he can be if you let him), he loves you, and he fights for you. So "Don't worry about a thing," and be at perfect peace.

EPILOGUE

It is my hope that this small simple book has given you a perspective of how you can move from panic to peace. Yes, it is a mindset but one coupled with practical applicable tools and tips. Just as staying in good physical condition takes work, staying in good mental and spiritual condition also takes work and practice. So be sure to review the contents of this manuscript again and again, employing it to help you achieve peace and stay at peace. May the words of the little birds' song ring true in your life now and forever as you keep before you the hopeful promise that when your life is Christ's "every little thing gonna be alright."

ABOUT THE AUTHOR

Gabriel O'Sullivan is a follower of Christ, husband, and father. He is happily married to his high school sweetheart, Ryanne. The couple have three wonderful children, Avery, Isaac, and Tyson. The family is active in their church, community, and local sports programs. Check out more content by Gabriel by reading his first book Thy Will Be Done? Trusting God in the Midst of Suffering, Pain, or Loss. You can also listen to the podcast Lost Boys to Found Fathers.